Little Guides to
Great Lives

AMELIA EARHART

to
Rowan

Marianna Madriz
18/06

Isbel Thomas

LAURENCE KING

Published in 2018
by Laurence King Publishing Ltd
361–373 City Road
London EC1V 1LR
United Kingdom
Tel: +44 20 7841 6900
E-mail: enquiries@laurenceking.com
www.laurenceking.com

Illustrations © 2018 Dàlia Adillon

A catalogue record for this book is available
from the British Library

ISBN: 978-1-78627-159-4

Commissioning Editor: Chloë Pursey
Senior Editor: Charlotte Selby
Design concept: Charlotte Bolton
Book design: The Urban Ant Ltd.

Printed in China

Other *Little Guides to Great Lives*:
Marie Curie
Charles Darwin
Frida Kahlo
Leonardo da Vinci
Nelson Mandela

Little Guides to
Great Lives

AMELIA
EARHART

Written by
Isabel Thomas

Illustrations by
Dàlia Adillon

Laurence King Publishing

Amelia Earhart was one of America's first superstars. She was mobbed by cheering crowds, made the front page of every newspaper and even launched her own fashion line.

Amelia wasn't a <u>politician</u>, a film star or a singer. She was ... an <u>aviator</u>!

Amelia made daring flights across land and sea. She wasn't the best female pilot in the world, but she was definitely the best-known.

Then, one day, Earhart disappeared as she flew over the Pacific Ocean. That was more than 80 years ago, and the mystery has still not been solved.

Amelia's story begins in a small town in Kansas, USA.

When Amelia was little, her family were very close. Amy read exciting stories to the girls. Edwin took them fishing and played ball games.

Amy Otis
(mother)

Edwin Stanton Earhart
(father)

Amelia Mary Earhart
known as 'Meeley'
Born 24 July 1897

Muriel Earhart
known as 'Pidge'
(sister)

They loved to explore and have adventures outdoors. When Amelia was seven she designed and built a rollercoaster in the garden.

Amelia grew up in the early 1900s, when the world was changing in exciting ways. Aeroplanes were a brand new invention!

The Wright brothers made the world's first powered flight in 1903 (Amelia was six).

Aeroplanes were soon the star attraction at fairs and festivals everywhere. Amelia first saw one at the Iowa State Fair, in 1908. She was not impressed.

"It was a thing of rusty wire and wood and not at all interesting."

So what did Amelia like?

Things I like

Reading about insects
Riding horses
Inventing things
Exciting adventures

Basketball
Mathematics
Celery

Things I hate

The way people expect boys to be better at stuff (I have jumped over a fence that no boy my age had dared to jump!)

Wearing dresses

Sweets

In the early 1900s, boys were expected to be adventurous and choose an exciting career. Girls were expected to learn sewing, music and good manners, then get married and look after children. Amelia decided this was not for her.

Amelia collected articles about women who were choosing a different path.

amelia

Life at home became harder for Amelia when she was in her teens. Her father lost his job and became an <u>alcoholic</u>. Her parents separated, and would later divorce. Amelia still loved her father, but sometimes she felt like she was the parent and he was the child.

Amelia dreamed of the time when her real life full of adventures would start. The problem was, she didn't know what she wanted to do.

One day, Amelia came across soldiers who had been wounded in World War One.

> "For the first time I realized what the World War meant. I saw ... men without arms and legs, men who were <u>paralyzed</u> and men who were blind."

Instead of finishing her school exams, Amelia decided to try and help. She moved to Toronto, Canada, and volunteered as a nurse until the war ended.

Amelia worked six days a week scrubbing floors, handing out medicine, serving meals, massaging cramps and playing games with patients ...

In Toronto, Amelia visited an <u>airfield</u> with her sister. A stunt pilot dived towards the girls for a joke but Amelia was not scared. She was hooked!

"I did not understand it at the time, but I believe that the little airplane said something to me as it swished by."

When the war finished, Amelia still wasn't sure what to do with her life. She began training as a doctor, but left to join her parents in California. She visited local air shows, and in 1920 she paid $10 to go up in a plane herself!

The flight over Los Angeles was the most exciting 10 minutes she'd ever had! Amelia knew she had to become a pilot herself.

There was just one problem ...

1 minute of ✈ = $1
1 hour of ✈ = $60
40 hours of ✈ = $2,400!

Amelia needed a job. She began working in her father's office, and took a second job sorting post in a telephone company.

She was soon ready to begin flying lessons and wanted to be taught by a female pilot. Amelia asked Anita Snook, an <u>aviation pioneer</u>. They became great friends.

Anita Snook

Call me Neta!

Amelia often made silly mistakes. Instead of '<u>flying by feel</u>' she liked to rely on her instruments. But she was never happier than when she was in the air.

Amelia took on more jobs to save up for lessons, fuel and her own plane! She worked as a truck driver, a photographer, a typist and a sausage seller, all while studying for her lessons.

After six months she had enough money to buy a shiny yellow <u>biplane</u>.

The *Canary*
Kinner Airster

She also had her first crash! But this was quite normal at the time. Flying was dangerous, engines sometimes stopped working, and wooden planes were fragile.

Amelia would have loads more bumps and bruises, but for her it was all part of the fun.

In 1921, Amelia passed the tests to get her National Aeronautic Association flying licence. Two years later she got her international pilot's licence.

Amelia was the sixteenth woman ever to get one of these!

Now she could take part in races – though she thought it was unfair that women weren't allowed to join the men's races.

Certificate No. 6017

This certifies that Amelia M. Earhart, born 24th day of July 1897, has fulfilled all the conditions required to be an Aviator Pilot.

Dated May 15, 1923

She even flew higher than a female pilot had ever flown – up to 14,000 feet!

After her parents divorced, Amelia moved to Boston with her mother and sister. She kept flying, but fuel was so expensive that she needed to keep working hard.

Amelia enjoyed helping people, so she became a social worker. She taught English to Syrian and Chinese families who had immigrated to America, and helped them to get settled. She organized games for children, and took them on outings.

She also spent time encouraging other women to use aeroplanes – and learn to fly themselves.

One day she got a call that would change her life.

Hello. Would you like to be the first woman to fly across the Atlantic?

Amelia had to pinch herself. A famous publisher called George Putman was looking for a woman brave enough to travel by plane across the Atlantic Ocean.

Planes were still small and unreliable, so it would be a tough and dangerous mission.

"I couldn't say no. I wanted to go because I love life and all it has to offer. I want every opportunity and adventure it can give."

On 17 June 1928, Amelia squeezed into the cabin of the *Friendship*, between two tanks of explosive fuel! The plane was flown by Wilmer Stultz and co-pilot Louis Gordon, so all Amelia had to do was look out of the window and write in her log book.

4,000 feet. More than three tons of us are hurtling through the air. We are in the storm now. Three tons is shaken considerably.

At 10,000 feet, above the clouds, but freezing cold. Water is dripping in at the windows. The engine sounds like it will cut out.

Just over 20 hours after taking off, the crew were relieved to see boats and finally ... land!

They touched down on 18 June 1928. They had been aiming for Ireland, but they had actually landed in Burry Port, South Wales!

They flew on to London and were met by cheering crowds.

Overnight, Amelia had become a superstar!
This meant:

- ♥ exciting offers
- ♥ a book deal
- ♥ invitations to give talks around the world
- ♥ <u>product endorsements</u>
- ♥ party invitations
- ♥ free stuff
- ♥ money (which she used to support her family)

George Putman helped her take advantage of every opportunity. Amelia even began writing for *Cosmopolitan* magazine. She used her talks and articles to tell women about the joys of flying, and to show that it was a safe form of transport.

She also wanted to show women that exciting adventures weren't just for men. Women could follow their dreams too.

Amelia Earhart
LUGGAGE

November
Cosmopolitan
35 Cents

20 Hrs. 40 Min.
Our Flight in
the Friendship

Amelia
Earhart

AMELIA
EARHART
Will Tell You All
You Want to Know
About FLYING

George dreamed up new challenges to keep Amelia on the front page of every newspaper. They included the Women's Air Derby – a coast-to-coast race across the USA, from California to Ohio. Twenty women pilots started the race ...

Claire Fahy's wing braces snapped.

Margaret Perry caught <u>typhoid fever</u>.

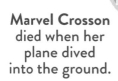

Thea Rasche found sand in her fuel tank but finished.

Marvel Crosson died when her plane dived into the ground.

Mary von Mach came ninth.

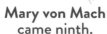

Bobbi Trout finished but was untimed.

Blanche Noyes' plane caught fire. She landed, put out the fire with desert sand, took off again and came fourth!

Gladys O'Donnell came second ...

Amelia flipped her plane over when she hit a ridge. It was fixed quickly and she came third.

Louise Thaden won!

Ruth Elder landed in a field of cows but came fifth.

... but only 15 pilots finished.

Amelia married George Putman, but she didn't settle down. Their plans became even more ambitious!

A few days after the Air Derby, Amelia called a meeting of women pilots. They decided to start the first organization for women aviators.

They had 99 applications to join, so they called themselves ... the Ninety-Nines.

Amelia also wanted to become the first woman to fly solo across the Atlantic Ocean.

The rest of the world thought she was bonkers. Seven women had died trying to do the same thing.

But Amelia wanted to prove to herself (and the world) that she wasn't just a passenger.

On 20 May 1932 she took off into the sunset.

It was not an easy journey.

Amelia had practised 'flying blind', relying on her instruments to tell her where her plane was. But four hours after taking off, her altimeter failed.

In thick fog and cloud, she had no way of knowing how high she was. Then she flew into a terrible storm. Wind, rain and lightning bashed the plane for an hour. She decided to keep going.

At one point she climbed too high, and ice formed on the plane. It plunged out of the sky, dropping 3,000 feet towards the ocean ...

... but Amelia wrestled with the controls, and brought it level again before she hit the water below.

After almost 15 hours of flying alone, Amelia was so happy to see land. She touched down in a field of cows.

Amelia had done it! She had flown 2,026 miles in 14 hours and 56 minutes!

Amelia had:

- ♥ Become the second person to fly the Atlantic solo
  (and the first woman!)
- ♥ Set a new record for the fastest crossing
- ♥ Made the longest non-stop flight by a woman

There was no time to rest. Amelia visited Paris,
London and Rome, collecting honours and awards.

Amelia accepted her awards on behalf of all women – flyers and non-flyers – and in her interviews, speeches and lectures she reminded people that women were the equals of men.

She was now the most famous American woman after the First Lady, Eleanor Roosevelt, and the two became good friends. Amelia launched a fashion line and began working for Purdue University, encouraging women to become <u>engineers</u>, scientists, doctors and business leaders.

She wanted all women to dream big.

Amelia
Earhart

Next, Amelia became the first pilot to fly across the Pacific Ocean from Hawaii to California – an 18-hour flight. She kept a log of the journey.

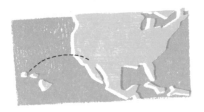

IN THE AIR

The night I found over the Pacific was a night of stars. They seemed to rise from the sea and hang outside my cockpit window, near enough to touch, until hours later they slipped away into the dawn.

TAKE-OFF

I saw several women with handkerchiefs obviously ready for any emergency. Out of the corner of my eye I sighted three fire engines and an ambulance posted down the field where 'X' might be expected to mark the spot if an accident occurred.

FOOD

What did I eat? My standard ration –
plain tomato juice, one hard-boiled egg,
and the most memorable cup of
hot chocolate I have ever had.

LANDING

This time I didn't have to explain who I was
when I landed. Thousands of people were
waiting to greet the plane. Cameras clicked as
soon as I opened the cockpit.

By 1937, Amelia was running out of records to break!

There was just one big prize left, that no woman or man had ever attempted ...

To fly around the world

at its widest point

Pilots, <u>mechanics</u> and <u>navigators</u> helped Amelia and George to plan a zigzag route covering more than 30,000 miles.

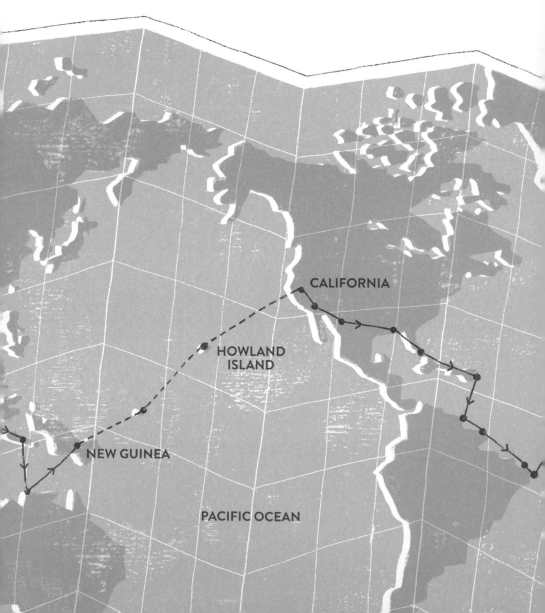

CALIFORNIA

HOWLAND
ISLAND

NEW GUINEA

PACIFIC OCEAN

Purdue University helped pay for a magnificent, all-metal plane that could fly 4,500 miles non-stop. Even President Roosevelt did what he could to help!

Amelia took off from California on 21 May, 1937, heading east. After 40 days she had travelled nearly 22,000 miles with more than 20 stops.

All she had to do now was cross the Pacific Ocean, from New Guinea to California. It was such a huge distance that she would have to stop on Howland Island to refuel. She took a navigator called Fred Noonan along, to help her find the tiny island in the middle of the world's biggest ocean.

Amelia and Fred took off from New Guinea on 2 July. It would take them about 20 hours to fly the 2,556 miles to Howland Island.

The Coast Guard boat *Itasca* waited near Howland Island to guide her in over the radio. But it soon became clear that radio signals to *Itasca* were not getting through ...

GMT

17.45   About 200 miles out. Approximately. Whistling now.

18.15   Please take bearing on us and report in half hour I will make noise in microphone – about 100 miles out

19.12   KAHQQ calling Itasca we must be on you but cannot see you but gas is running low been unable to reach you by radio we are flying at <u>altitude</u> 1,000 feet

19.29   We are circling but cannot hear you go ahead on 7,500 either now or on the schedule time on half hour

19.30   KHAQQ calling Itasca we received your signals but unable to get a minimum please take bearing on us and answer 3105 with voice

20.14   We are on the line on position 157-337, will repeat this message on 6,210 kcs. Wait, listening on 6,210 kcs. We are running north and south

And then ... silence.

Amelia's disappearance made front-page news around the world.

THE NEWS

EARHART PLANE LOST AT SEA

Amelia Earhart Missing on World Flight

The Daily Chronical

AMELIA EARHART DOWN AT SEA
WARSHIP CATCHES FAINT SIGNAL!

The Times

AMELIA FEARED LOST!

MISS EARHART FORCED DOWN AT SEA, HOWLAND ISLE FEARS. COAST GUARD BEGINS SEARCH

NAVY HUNTS AMELIA LOST IN PACIFIC OCEAN

The *Itasca* searched for Amelia's plane for 17 days. It was joined by ships from the USA, Britain and Japan, 60 aeroplanes and more than 4,000 people.

Together they combed more than 250,000 square miles of ocean, and dozens of small islands. George Putman kept searching until October. But Amelia, Fred and their plane were never found.

What happened to Amelia Earhart?

Many theories have been put forward since she disappeared. Here are some of them ...

She could not spot the tiny island because it was hidden under clouds.

Crashed and sank, dying instantly.

Ran out of fuel and had to land on the shark-infested ocean.

Let me out!

This is Amelia Earhart. Help me!

Water's knee deep!

Crashed near a beach on Buka Island (some people claimed to hear radio messages from Amelia for five days after she disappeared).

Eaten alive by foot-long centipedes and giant crabs on Nikumaroro.

Got 'lost' on purpose because she was actually working as a spy, to map the Pacific for the US Navy.

Faked her death, changed her identity and lived as a housewife called Irene Bolam until her late 70s.

Landed in the Marshall Islands by mistake, was captured by Japanese soldiers and taken to a prison in Saipan, where she died of <u>dysentery</u>.

In January 1939, Amelia was declared legally dead.

She was one of the most famous women in the world when she died, and 80 years later, she is still famous.

New technology has made it possible to search a huge area of ocean near Howland Island with <u>submersibles</u> and <u>sonar</u>, but no trace of Amelia's plane has been found.

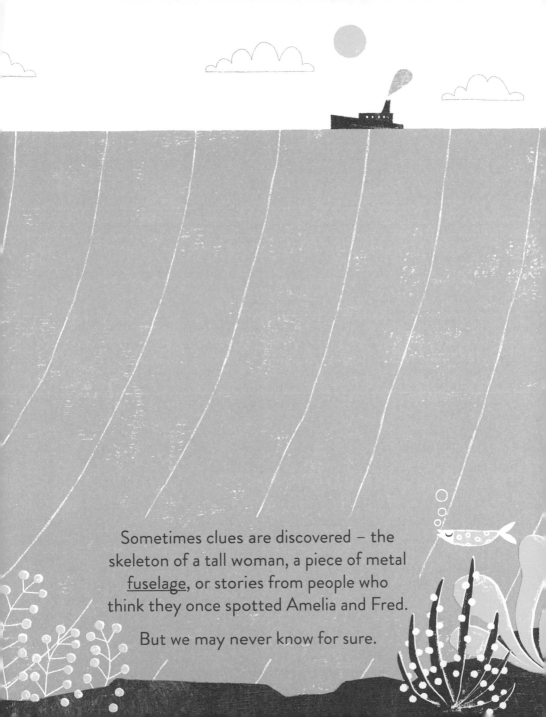

Sometimes clues are discovered – the skeleton of a tall woman, a piece of metal <u>fuselage</u>, or stories from people who think they once spotted Amelia and Fred.

But we may never know for sure.

Amelia was daring and determined. She worked hard to show girls and women they could be anything they wanted to be, and do anything they wanted to do.

That's why she is remembered – not just for the mysterious way she died, but for the amazing way that she lived.

"Whether it was considered the thing
to do or not was irrelevant.
As a little girl I had explored the
fearsome caves in the cliffs, I had invented
a trap and caught a chicken, I had
jumped over a fence that no boy my age had
dared to jump, and I knew there was
more fun and excitement in life than
I would have time to enjoy."

Things Amelia did in <u>aviation</u>:

Set a women's altitude record
(14,000 feet)

First woman to cross
Atlantic Ocean by air
as a passenger

Set women's speed
record over 3 km
(181.18 mph)

Set women's flying
speed record over
100 km (174.897 mph)

Set altitude
record in an
<u>autogyro</u>
(18,451 feet)

First person to
make solo return
flight across USA
in an autogyro

First person to
fly solo across the
Pacific Ocean
from Hawaii to
California

First woman to make
a solo return air flight
across the USA

Became a role model
for women

First president of
the Ninety-Nines

Helped attract passengers
to America's first
commercial airlines

Wrote two books,
20 Hrs. 40 Min.
and *The Fun of It*

First person to
cross the Atlantic
twice by air

First woman to
fly solo across the
Atlantic Ocean

First person to fly
solo from Los Angeles
to Mexico City

Set women's record
for fastest non-stop
transcontinental flight

TIMELINE

1897
Amelia is born on 24 July in Atchison, Kansas, USA. Her parents are Samuel 'Edwin' Stanton Earhart and Amelia 'Amy' Otis Earhart. Amelia's nickname was 'Meeley'.

1899
Amelia's sister Grace Muriel Earhart is born. Her nickname is 'Pidge'.

1903
The Wright brothers complete the world's first powered flight.

1917
Amelia moves to Toronto, Canada, and volunteers as a nurse during World War One at a hospital.

1919
Amelia moves to Northampton, Massachusetts, and begins training as a doctor.

1920
Amelia leaves university and moves to California. She experiences her first flight with Frank Hawks and becomes determined to learn to fly.

1925
Amelia works as a social worker in Boston, Massachusetts.

1928
In June, Amelia becomes the first woman to fly across the Atlantic Ocean as a passenger.

1929
Amelia's overnight fame means exciting offers, invitations and money. She comes third in the Women's Air Derby from California to Ohio.

1935
Amelia is the first woman to fly solo across the Pacific. She is named America's Outstanding Airwoman.

1935
Amelia begins working with Purdue University, which also helps provide the money for her to buy an aeroplane to make a round-the-world trip.

1937
In June, Amelia begins her round-the-world flight from Florida. On 2 July, Amelia and Fred disappear near Howland Island. The coast guard searches for Amelia's plane for 17 days.

1908
Amelia sees an aeroplane for the first time at the Iowa State Fair.

1910
The Earhart sisters are educated at home by their mother and a governess until Amelia is 12 years old, when she starts going to the Hyde Park High School in Chicago.

1916
Amelia graduates from Hyde Park High School at the age of 18.

1921
Amelia begins flying lessons with Anita 'Neta' Snook and then purchases her first aircraft, the Kinner Airster she named the *Canary*.

1922
Amelia sets a world record for women's flying with an altitude record of 14,000 feet.

1923
Amelia becomes the sixteenth woman to be issued a pilot's licence.

1930
Amelia sets the women's world flying speed record at 181.18 mph over a 3-km course in July and gets her air transport licence in October.

1931
Amelia is elected as the first president of the Ninety-Nines (women's pilot association). She marries George Putman and he becomes her manager.

1932
In May, Amelia becomes the first woman to fly solo across the Atlantic. In August, Amelia becomes the first woman to fly non-stop across USA and breaks the speed record. Amelia's book is published.

1939
In January, Amelia is declared legally dead. Her disappearance remains an unsolved mystery.

Amelia Earhart

GLOSSARY

airfield – an area of land set aside for the take-off, landing and maintenance of aircraft.

alcoholic – a person who suffers from an addiction to alcohol.

altimeter – an instrument used by pilots to measure the altitude.

altitude – the height of an object in relation to sea level or ground level.

autogyro – a form of aircraft with horizontal blades and a propeller.

aviation – the flying or operating of aircraft.

aviation pioneer – a person directly and indirectly responsible for the advancement of flight, including people who achieved significant 'firsts' in aviation.

aviator – a pilot.

biplane – an early type of aircraft with two pairs of wings, one above the other.

dysentery – an infection of the intestines which causes severe diarrhoea.

engineer – a person who designs, constructs and tests structures, materials and systems.

flying blind – a term which was originally used by pilots, meaning relying on an aircraft's instruments because the visibility is poor. The term is now used more widely, meaning doing something new without any help or instructions.

flying by feel – a term used by pilots, meaning being able to fly an aircraft without relying heavily on the aircraft's instruments.

fuselage – the main body of an aircraft.

mechanic – a person who repairs and

maintains vehicle engines and other machines.

navigator – a person who plans and directs the route of a ship, aircraft or other form of transport, using instruments or maps.

paralyzed – the loss of the ability to move (and sometimes feel anything) in part or most of the body, typically as a result of illness, poison or injury.

politician – a person who works in politics, which is the governing of a country or area.

product endorsements – when a celebrity or business is paid to recommend a product.

social worker – a person whose job helps individuals, families, groups and communities to improve their wellbeing and to help them develop their own skills to resolve problems.

sonar – a system used to find objects under water by producing sound pulses and detecting or measuring their return after being reflected.

submersible – a small boat that can operate underwater, often used for research and exploration.

typhoid fever – a bacterial infection that can spread throughout the body. Without fast treatment, it can cause serious problems and may kill the person.

INDEX

CREDITS

Photograph on page 61 courtesy of the Library of Congress